7/09

D1622107

HIGH-RISK
CONSTRUCTION WORK

Life Building Skyscrapers, Bridges, and Tunnels

Philip Wolny

Marion Carnegie Library
206 S. Market St.
Marion, IL 62959

rosen publishing's
rosen
central®

New York

For my father, who paid his dues as a contractor

Published in 2009 by The Rosen Publishing Group, Inc.
29 East 21st Street, New York, NY 10010

Copyright © 2009 by The Rosen Publishing Group, Inc.

First Edition

All rights reserved. No part of this book may be reproduced in any form without permission in writing from the publisher, except by a reviewer.

Library of Congress Cataloging-in-Publication Data

Wolny, Philip.
High-risk construction work: life building skyscrapers, bridges, and tunnels / Philip Wolny.
        p. cm. — (Extreme careers)
Includes bibliographical references and index.
ISBN-13: 978-1-4042-1789-8 (library binding)
1. Structural engineering—Juvenile literature. 2. Skyscrapers—Juvenile literature. 3. Bridges—Juvenile literature. 4. Tunnels—Juvenile literature. 5. Building—Vocational guidance—Juvenile literature. I. Title.
TA634.W65 2009
624.1—dc22
                                                      2007042996

Manufactured in Malaysia

Contents

Introduction

Imagine yourself standing on the edge of a building hundreds of feet up in the air. It is morning, the sky is blue, and the air is breezy. You can see almost a hundred miles in every direction. The sun reflects brilliantly off the steel beams in your view. You double-check the safety harness you're wearing before carefully making your way across narrow scaffolding. A new day beckons.

Or, imagine yourself twenty feet (six meters) deep in a trench or in a darkened tunnel. You use heavy machines to drill through damp earth and rock. The deeper you go, the farther away you are from the outside world.

Whether high above or down below, the job of the construction worker is one of the most interesting and important existing occupations. Unless you live in a tent in the middle of the forest, the end products of construction work are everywhere around you. Structures such as buildings, bridges, and roads are some of the basic elements of modern life. Every day, hundreds of thousands of workers wake up to a day of hard but rewarding work.

Construction work has the potential to be one of the more dangerous jobs out there. The hands-on aspects of the work make it an extreme career. One needs to be physically fit and mentally able, and must use common sense at all times. Whether it's completing a project on time or looking ahead to create a safe environment for everyone, construction is not a career for the absent-minded or faint of heart.

A construction worker balances high above the city while hammering a rivet into a steel beam.

A Hands-On Career

Building has been important to civilizations for thousands of years. It is only in the last two hundred years or so, however, that we have seen the construction industry develop as we know it. Most large-scale projects are now broken up into two sectors. One is commercial building, which includes office towers, apartment buildings, and shopping centers. The other is public works, such as subway tunnels, bridges, and public utilities. While private companies are usually in charge of commercial buildings, governments usually lead public works projects. Still, governments often hire private companies as contractors for specific aspects of a job.

A Rewarding Job

What is the appeal of construction work? There are many reasons to be attracted to construction as a career. It's a "hands-on" career, meaning it involves working with one's hands a great deal. The work can sometimes be grueling, but it is

Wearing a helmet, life jacket, and safety harness, a worker crouches on a wooden plank as he works on a bridge above Chesapeake Bay in Norfolk, Virginia.

physically and mentally satisfying. As they build, workers can step back and take in their progress. They can touch and feel what they are building, and they see the physical product of their labor develop and grow.

Variety is another attractive quality of this line of work. No two days are the same. Some projects, like big office and residential buildings, or large underground projects, such as subway tunnels and sewers, may take months or years to complete. The famous "Big Dig" in Boston, Massachusetts, which rerouted highway traffic through an underground tunnel, is an extreme example of a long project—it continued for almost

Women Breaking Down Walls

While construction work traditionally has been considered a male profession due to the job's physical demands, many more women are entering the construction industry than ever before. Pamela Novotny, for example, a mother of three, started working in bridge construction at the age of forty-four. According to a July 2006 interview in the *New Hampshire Business Review*, Novotny was attracted to construction work because her father worked thirty-five years as a crane operator. She finally got her chance through New Hampshire's state-run On the Job training program. By the time of her interview, she already had four hundred hours of training in bridge construction. She enjoys her job and said, "I love having the chance to work at something different every day. That, and the physical work . . . [working] outside, . . . and to really be able to use my hands and get them dirty. You really feel like you've accomplished something at the end of the day." She admitted that the challenging part of the job was that "there's so much to learn . . . It can be tough trying to take it all in. But that's also the coolest thing about this job."

two decades! However, even on a lengthy job or a big project, construction workers often deal with a great variety of work and move around their work sites. Other construction workers may deal with a single aspect of building a structure and then move on to another.

Many construction workers are drawn to the job because they don't like sitting at a desk in front of a computer for long periods of time. For them, a highly attractive aspect is the chance to work outside instead of looking at the same four walls for eight hours a day.

Many Job Options

There are many jobs that fall under the construction-work umbrella. It's a large industry. According to the U.S. Census Bureau, in the United States alone, it is estimated that as much as $768 billion was spent on construction in the first eight months of 2007. It is also an ever-expanding industry, both in the United States and worldwide. Therefore, the demand for workers is constantly growing.

As her instructor looks on, an engineering student marks blueprints at a construction site. The presence of women in the construction industry is growing steadily.

Construction work requires a vast array of skills. Many construction workers, especially those starting out, work as general laborers and do a variety of jobs. Others are specialists in a particular skill or trade, such as carpenters, pipe fitters, and bricklayers. Workers often start off in one aspect of the job and move into another. Many construction workers find that their jobs contain an appealing mix of hard labor, engineering, administration, and other tasks.

A Living Wage

A good salary also makes construction work an attractive career option. Even laborers who are relatively unskilled or inexperienced make a decent wage. As they gain experience and skills through training or schooling, wages increase. More responsibility also leads to more money.

Working for some companies can be seasonal, or there might be periodic breaks from work, especially between construction projects. Depending on a project deadline, however, the days can start early and end late. Many workers don't mind this because construction workers are generally paid for overtime. A rate of "time and a half," or 1.5 times the normal hourly rate, is standard overtime pay. For most jobs, especially if a worker is part of a labor union, overtime starts after a worker has worked forty hours per week. For nonunion workers, overtime rates may vary depending on the employer.

The Chance to Grow

Making a good salary is always attractive. But many construction workers like the industry for reasons aside from money. Self-improvement is a big aspect of a construction career. Workers who want to grow in their careers have that opportunity. Those who get to the top and look for new goals and challenges can find them. Some become project managers. Others start their own companies, using their experiences to lead others. For the many laborers who teach apprentices, the chance to pass on their knowledge and wisdom to another generation of workers can also be satisfying.

What It Takes

What does it take to be a construction worker? For one, you need to have a desire to create something and leave a visible mark on the world. As with any career, you need to be sure it is something

Construction demands both physical and mental ability. Here, a construction worker uses his laptop on-site at a condominium development.

you have a knack for and want to do. Otherwise, you won't last very long.

Physically, you need to be good with your hands. If you prefer building the sets for the school play to being the lead actor, for example, that already tells you something. Clumsy people or people who don't enjoy making things are likely ill-suited to work as laborers. Taking trade courses or drafting during high school are good ways to figure out if you have what it takes. Most important, these courses let you discover whether you really enjoy such work.

Strength and Stamina

It's not just mechanical aptitude that makes a good construction worker. Physical conditioning is also key. Carrying heavy loads is customary, as is holding up a heavy object while someone

Two construction workers hoist a support beam into place while on a job in Centreville, Virginia. Construction demands not only physical strength and stamina but also agility and the ability to communicate and work well together.

else works on it. Sitting and crouching in various uncomfortable positions for long stretches of time are common. Construction workers need stamina and endurance as well as strength. That means they must have the ability to withstand physical exertion. It is stamina that keeps a boxer going through a long match or helps a runner finish a 26-mile (41.8 kilometer) marathon.

Strong in Mind and Body

Mental stamina and agility are as much a part of the job as physical stamina. You have to think fast on your feet. As with any job where there are deadlines, there is the stress of getting things done on time. Holdups make life harder on everyone else. Still, accidents and other unforeseen events can occur, and they might set back a project by hours, days, weeks, or even months. Figuring out ways to get back on schedule takes sharpness and imagination. When you have to work more quickly, you also have to think extra hard about safety. Hurrying often results in making careless mistakes. And in a construction environment, even the most minor mistakes can mean disaster. Making a mistake on a marketing project might mean getting in trouble with the boss, but putting up a wall improperly could mean a fatal collapse. Any number of workers could be gravely, or even fatally, injured.

According to a study on workplace fatalities published in 2006 by the U.S. Bureau of Labor Statistics (BLS), nearly 1,190 construction workers died on the job in 2005. However, construction workers ranked after fishermen, loggers, and pilots in terms of dangerous occupations. Unlike fishermen, who suffer 114 deaths per 100,000 workers annually, construction-related deaths were about 11 per 100,000 workers. (This number of deaths is due to the fact that there are so many construction workers to begin with.) Still, safety is improving every year.

"Work Smarter, Not Harder"

"Work smarter, not harder" is a frequent battle cry in construction work. Someone who can think ahead and foresee problems will always do better than someone who is thinking only about the present. A construction project is a team effort. Even the leaders of the project won't be able to predict everything that could go wrong. It's often the workers on the site that contribute valuable information and suggestions.

Off to Work We Go!

Many people make the mistake of thinking of construction as mindless physical labor. However, there are many career paths in construction work. Laborers must have some degree of literacy and mathematic ability in order to do the job at a competent level. Anyone who wants to advance beyond a certain point also needs the ability to learn and adapt to ever-changing situations. New and more advanced construction machinery and techniques are constantly introduced.

Some people have formal training before they start working in construction. They take classes, and they may even participate in an apprenticeship. Others get into the field in a less formal way. They might get a job doing construction work right out of high school and find that they love it. A college student might work summers in construction. Others have relatives or family in the industry who inspire them or recommend them for work. Once they get a taste of the construction life, they may find that it suits them.

High school classes, including drafting, wood shop, and metal shop, can be a good way to learn some building basics. Above, a student at Fowler High School in Syracuse, New York, uses a drill press to make part of a wooden toy.

High School Classes

The minimum education a construction worker needs is usually a high school diploma. While not everyone has one (and many foreign-born workers who are undocumented lack one), a high school or GED (General Educational Development) diploma is generally required.

If you decide in high school that you want to work in construction, there are classes you should look to take. Drafting or technical drawing classes are a great idea. These get you accustomed to precision and familiar with the technical aspects of the career. Wood shop or metal shop classes are also highly recommended. They are a good way to learn building basics and discover the fun and accomplishment of designing and completing small projects. You can also find out if there is a high school in your area that specializes in construction. These schools are generally known as technical high schools. They stress math and engineering as well as skills for different trades. (Trades are the different types of skilled labor in which workers can specialize, including carpentry, electrical work, and metal work.) These kinds of schools also usually have contacts with companies and government agencies that employ construction laborers.

If you don't have such schools or classes in your area, you might want to look for a summer or after-school job helping out at a construction firm. Due to strict labor laws, you probably won't be able to do any hands-on work. You might run errands, help clean up, and do a variety of other tasks. This kind of job will give you invaluable exposure as to how a construction sight looks, feels, and runs.

Once you graduate from high school, whether it's a technical or a regular school, there's a whole world of possibilities for a construction worker.

Higher Learning

If you plan on going beyond the career of a general laborer, you might explore applying to college programs. There are programs in civil engineering and construction management, for example, among other majors. After graduation, you will be ready to work on projects with a minimum of on-the-job training. It is often fairly competitive to enter these kinds of college programs, and the pace of learning is rather intense. You need good grades to be admitted, and you must do well to stay in the program. College students specializing in construction learn construction-related math as well as a variety of subjects ranging from the proper use of materials and methods of construction to planning, scheduling, and accounting.

Learning on the Job

The most informal way of learning construction work is to learn "on the job." After you're hired, you basically show up and do what you're told. You watch others and learn from them. When possible, you ask questions, and often, more experienced workers will be able to help you. You also learn by doing. Even if the tasks are confusing or complicated, repetition makes things more and more familiar over time. While of course your goal is to avoid making mistakes, it's inevitable that you will make some. Don't beat yourself up over them. Instead, learn from them and take them as the lessons they are.

When learning on the job, one generally starts off as a helper. Typical duties for a helper might include transporting and loading materials. Helpers may also clean and prepare a site for other workers. In other words, they do the dirty work

A carpenter *(right)* and his apprentice work on a bridge over the Grand River in Lansing, Michigan. Mentors and other experienced colleagues can be a great resource for workers when they're just starting out in the field.

that requires few skills. But the longer they are around, the more responsibilities helpers are given. They get chances to use some of the simpler equipment and tools. Their responsibilities grow continually.

The Apprentice

Apprenticeships are a popular and helpful way to get into construction work. Instead of learning informally on the job, you get a structured education while earning your keep on construction sites. Typically, you are assigned to one or more mentors within a particular specialty. Thus, there are apprentice carpenters, apprentice bricklayers, apprentice electricians, and so forth.

One advantage to most apprenticeships is that they take two to four years to complete. Getting those same skills without an apprenticeship often takes longer if you learn on the job as a helper. Still, there are a limited number of apprenticeships offered annually in any given area, in any given industry specialty. These are not filled randomly: usually, you need to show that you've gotten good grades in high school or at other schools you have attended. As with any job, you may have to make it through one or several interviews to get the position.

Apprenticeships are frequently offered by trade unions that specialize in a particular skill, often in partnership with private construction companies. Apprenticeships aren't just good for the workers who are learning. They are to the benefit of the industry as a whole. Much of construction work is autonomous; in other words, workers basically do their jobs without someone looking over everything they do. Therefore bosses initially need to be sure that everyone knows what they're doing. Thus, the standards are high for those completing an apprenticeship. Apprenticeships allow trainers to closely watch their apprentices' progress. It is a good way to produce skilled workers.

The apprentice completing the program learns a lifelong skill that can be used pretty much worldwide. Generally, after an apprenticeship it is quicker and easier to find a job. Often it

Looking for a Few Good People

Derek Burfect is an ironworker in Tacoma, Washington. During the third year of a four-year internship, he told the *Seattle Weekly* that he hadn't planned on construction as a career until he saw an advertisement in a local paper. A union, the Pacific Northwest Ironworkers and Employers, was looking for new employees. He responded to the ad, and now that he has some job experience, he's making great money. In fact, Burfect often tries to get friends into the business.

Surprisingly, the average age for beginning apprentices is twenty-eight. "Kids come out of high school and they bounce around for ten years," John Littel of the Seattle/King County Building and Construction Trades Council told the *Seattle Weekly*, adding that they come around when they realize that construction can be a satisfying and lucrative choice. Littel attends job fairs, trying to recruit graduating high school seniors to join the construction industry. He says they're surprised to hear that he makes up to $60 an hour while working on a site.

is possible to get a job through the same union or with the same company. There is also a greater choice of creative and exciting opportunities after completing an apprenticeship. With some apprenticeships, you even have enough training to start your own business.

Trade unions are one of the industry's most important training resources. Above, at the Carpenters Union training center in Fairfield, California, apprentices learn techniques to construct a building frame.

The Bureau of Apprenticeship Training

The federal government has an office that oversees apprenticeships nationwide. The Bureau of Apprenticeship Training, part of the U.S. Department of Labor, enforces apprenticeship standards. Usually, it requires registered apprenticeships to include at least one year or 2,000 hours of on-the-job training. It also recommends at least 144 hours of formal instruction. In most cases, an apprentice needs to be at least sixteen years of age, even if he or she has graduated early or already earned a GED.

Bottom of the Ladder?

As with any entry-level job, an apprenticeship can include a great deal of work. Nevada highway construction worker Cristy Riker started as a flagger, a person who directs traffic while construction is being done on a road. To get work year-round, Riker decided to join her local union, through which she received her appren-

A flagger directs motorists to slow down as they pass by a road project.

ticeship. Though she earns a bit less due to the fact that she must pay union dues, her apprenticeship will open doors to more skilled work and better pay in the future. She has had some tough jobs, but she has been learning a great deal. She told the *Reno Gazette Journal*, "The great thing about being an apprentice is that being trained, when wintertime comes, I can be working. I could shovel. I could sweep. I could go with

Gaining valuable technical and safety experience is a must for tough jobs like high-rise steel work. For these workers above the streets of midtown Manhattan in New York City, skill and safety are essential.

the concrete crew. It's all what I learned as an apprentice." One of the most important things to learn about just starting out is that *every* job is vital. Riker said, "I get a lot of people thinking I'm doing nothing as I stand there directing traffic. This is a very mental job. If I take my focus off for a split second, that opens up the door to hazard."

Where to Find Work

Generally, construction is a locally based business. Workers often find jobs that are a reasonable distance from their homes.

You may work quite steadily for one company for a long time. Or you might find yourself working for a few different companies on many different projects. In some cases, you may have to relocate or find temporary housing to follow a project far away from home. Depending on where you live, however, there may not be a great deal of construction work available. If not, you might want to consider moving to a large metro-politan area where work is easier to find.

Perilous Depths, Dizzying Heights

3

Not all construction work is the same. A worker's daily activities differ depending on where his or her work takes place. However, from deep underground to the greatest heights on a skyscraper, one thing is certain: a construction worker's day is full of many adventures and challenges.

Down Below: Tunnel Workers

Up above, heavy machines and buildings reach into the sky. A lot of construction work, however, is done beneath the ground's surface. Sewers, foundations for buildings, and trenches for pipes or electrical lines are just some of the big jobs that lead construction workers underground. It can be an interesting place to work, but it has its own rules and dangers.

Sandhogs: Heroes Out of Sight

In any major city or urban area, there is a whole underground world that few know very much about. In New York City, for

Chris Fitzsimmons, pictured 600 feet (183 m) below ground, is one of New York City's "sandhogs." Fitzsimmons and others are using powerful machinery to bore through bedrock beneath the streets of Manhattan in order to replace the water supply system.

example, the subways, sewers, and tunnels that bring water into the city for millions of residents were all created with the help of people who sometimes affectionately call themselves "sandhogs." (They got this name from the sand and other materials removed from under the ground.) Their work might include excavation, or the removal of materials from the earth. These "urban miners" create tunnels and passageways. Many of the projects they work on can last years, even decades.

Different rules apply underground, and tunnel work is an entirely unique experience, according to many sandhogs. Boston union leader Ken MacLean told the construction newsletter *Lifelines*, "It takes a different kind of person to be a tunneler." Talking about the first time he experienced tunnel work, he recalled workers using explosives to break up some tough rock. "Next thing, the blast of air was whizzing by, the adrenaline was rushing, and I was hooked." Tunneling is "hard, tough work," according to Ron Myers, another union representative. "You'd be surprised how many men—and women—can't take being confined underground like that."

Most tunnel workers train on the job, and employers tend to hire workers who already have previous experience in some kind of construction, said Richard Fitzsimmons, a New York City union leader. Fitzsimmons, who comes from a family of tunnel workers, agreed that "tunnelers are a unique breed."

The dangers of tunnel work are certainly unique. The confined spaces make access to oxygen a potential problem, with special enormous blowers bringing in air when needed. Tunnel workers keep careful track of who comes into and goes out of a tunnel site. This is because, unlike most outdoor construction work, underground laborers are often not visible to one another. If everyone isn't kept track of, a hurt or unconscious worker can escape notice. Fire is also a serious possible hazard, especially as it can travel quickly in enclosed spaces. Often standing in water, tunnel workers must be extra careful to avoid slipping and falling as well as possible electrocution.

If something does go wrong, it can often take a while to get help to an underground worker or to evacuate someone who is injured. Fitzsimmons said, "We have to know first aid and CPR.

Rescue procedures are also critical." Working so deep underground, a few minutes can mean the difference between life
and death.

Buried Alive

One of the dangers of working in tunnels is the danger of tunnel
collapses. It can be a frightening situation for everyone involved,
and it demands quick action on the part of rescuers. In August
2007, NBC news reported that a worker in Woodbridge, New
Jersey, was digging a trench to connect a building to a sewage
outlet. Suddenly, three separate dirt and mud collapses pinned
him down, burying him up to his neck.

Rescue workers jumped into action, but it took nearly four
hours to free him. In the end, it was discovered that supports had
not been placed in the trench to keep surrounding earth and
rock from caving in. Luckily, the worker was fine. Everyone
watching was reminded of the protection and care needed
during a dig.

Tunnel or trench collapse injuries are often fatal, since
workers are covered up in the blink of an eye. There are many
reasons a trench can collapse. A machine working too near the
edge of a support wall may cause a collapse. A recent hard
rain could shift the gravel, soil, or rock in a tunnel, trench, or
surrounding area.

Even rescuing someone who has fallen into a hole is not
necessarily simple. Done improperly, it can make things worse.
Placing or using rescue equipment incorrectly, or not being

When trenches collapse, workers can be completely buried in several feet of mud and dirt within a few seconds. Above, emergency personnel provide a trapped worker with oxygen as they work to dig him out of a collapsed trench.

careful around a hole where a worker has fallen, can cause a collapse. It is therefore possible to further endanger the trapped person or even the rescuers. An unidentified eighteen-year-old construction worker in Elverta, California, knows this first-hand. He fell 35 feet (10.7 m) down a hole in January 2007. Fortunately, the narrowness of the hole eased his fall, and he was able to use the walls to slow his drop.

As one coworker, Richard Snell, told the local ABC news affiliate, "He said he was okay. He wanted a rope to climb back out and we told him no, you wait for the fire department." When the firefighters arrived, they began by pumping oxygen to the worker, since a person in a hole can quickly use up breathable air. Eventually, they got the man out. Snell and his coworkers had made a good call. "Our biggest concern was collapse or cave-in," a fireman said at the scene.

Heavy Equipment Operator

The men and women operating the powerful machines at a construction site are usually called heavy equipment operators. Those that are trained to use several different kinds of machines, such as cranes and bulldozers, are sometimes called operating engineers. Work might include moving materials such as pipes, huge piles of dirt and rocks, or blocks of concrete. Other equipment is used to clear land and flatten it out so that construction can begin. Still other machines are used to dig trenches or to get to pipelines. Heavy equipment operators also run machinery

Operating heavy equipment, such as the backhoe pictured here, is one of the many important construction jobs. The heavy materials involved—and the tremendous power of the machines—make safety a top priority.

that pours asphalt or concrete onto roads or other structures. Sometimes they utilize pumps that drain water out of an area or powerful machinery that can support roofs or even entire buildings.

While everyone on a work site needs to be careful, operating engineers in particular must embrace safety. The strength and weight of the equipment, and the huge loads they handle, are awesome indeed. A wrong move could result in a thousand-pound (454 kilogram) wall tilting in the wrong direction, or a stack of concrete blocks spilling onto a coworker.

Therefore, safety training for operating engineers is extremely important. It's also important that other workers are careful around these machines. An asphalt paver can literally flatten a car beneath it; imagine what it could do to a human body! The same goes for other vehicles, like bulldozers. Sometimes, a piece of heavy machinery is the only thing standing between workers and disaster.

A Bridge Collapse: Victims and Heroes

In December 2003, the *San Francisco Chronicle* wrote about a bridge collapse north of San Francisco, California, on the Napa River. A hydraulic jack—a much bigger version of the jack that might be used to lift a car up in order to change a tire—slipped out from under its load. Steel beams and tons of wood that had been supporting two structures came raining down, burying the jack's operator, Travis Dewater.

Amazingly, he was able to dodge the worst of the debris, and the steel beams missed him. Crawling out from under the mess, bruised and battered but not badly injured, Dewater went to the aid of his coworkers. Workers and rescue teams that later arrived helped many workers, including a man who held onto a section of bridge, 75 feet (22.9 m) in midair, for over an hour before he was rescued. Sadly, however, one worker perished and several more were injured. Some of them were the workers that had been standing atop the bridge sections when it collapsed.

Tough Customers

The nature of construction work means that heavy equipment operators are working outside most of the time. They're usually hot in the summer and cold in the winter. In addition, they are often dirty from the mud, dust, and other elements with which they come into contact. On rare occasions, conditions like extreme rain will stop work if it becomes too difficult or dangerous. Still, heavy equipment operators are used at almost all stages of a project and in many different kinds of projects.

Heavy equipment operators need to be in good physical shape. They also need a good sense of a balance and the ability to judge distance accurately. Good eye-hand-foot coordination is necessary to properly operate the machinery, which can be complicated. Some operator positions require workers that are comfortable with heights.

On Top of the World

Construction workers build everywhere, from the very depths of the world to dizzying heights. When it comes to big projects like skyscrapers, workers have to be on top of things—literally.

The life of the high-rise construction laborer presents its own set of challenges. Like heavy equipment operators, good balance and an ability to work at great heights are crucial. Tripping on a wire or slipping on a misplaced tool can be bad enough at ground level. But higher up, the stakes are higher, too. There

This worker, high above ground, is putting together scaffolding with the help of a crane. His safety harness is an important first line of defense against falling. Still, he must keep his wits about him at all times.

is even less room for error. Failing to clean up a wet spot, leaving loose materials behind, and other oversights can have dire consequences.

Hot Enough for You?

High-rise laborers are also at the mercy of the weather, especially when it comes to the heat. A CNN reporter visited workers high up on a site in St. Louis, Missouri, in August 2007. A landlocked city with many brick buildings, St. Louis traps heat like a greenhouse. One worker told the reporter that he drank plenty of water and ate fruit every day to stay hydrated. The project manager on the site,

Dennis Jenkins, working on a baseball stadium in Washington, D.C., cools off by using his hard hat to dump water on his head.

Bob Herr, told CNN that the worst heat was "on the exterior of the building . . . because that's where you get the heat reflected off the building."

Hanging On

You might imagine that a huge danger involved with working on high-rises is related to the height itself, and you would be right. According to the Bureau of Labor Statistics' last extensive

A Whole World of Work

There are many different kinds of workers involved in large construction projects. Here are just a few of the workers' jobs:

Ironworkers

Despite the name, the workers in this highly skilled trade use iron, steel, and other metals. The materials are used to create structures' basic skeletons.

Welders

Often dressed from head to toe in protective gear, welders use open flame or electric tools to join pieces of metal by melting them together. Welders work everywhere—on steel frames of buildings and bridges, as well as deep in tunnels, welding pieces of pipeline together.

Carpenters

Carpenters work wherever they are needed. Using wood, they create interior walls, reinforce ceilings, build floors, put in doors, and work on dozens of other kinds of jobs.

Electricians

Electricians plan how electrical power will flow through a building. They carefully put in the wire, transformers, circuit breakers, and other equipment to get the power to where it can be used. The chance of falling, being cut, and electric shock make it one of the most dangerous construction jobs.

study, falls accounted for 33 percent of construction-related deaths in 2004. Still, it doesn't necessarily take a long fall to seriously hurt or kill a worker.

And even if you are extra careful, you can't plan for everything. That's something that Joseph Endico from New York City learned the hard way. He was standing on scaffolding, installing waterproofing on the third floor of an apartment complex. He was wearing a safety harness and a rope grab, a piece of line that attaches a worker to a rope as a backup safety device.

He told the *Gotham Gazette* that he could not recall hearing the sound of the rope snapping or noticing that his safety harness had failed. Endico realized he had fallen three stories to the ground below only after he had regained consciousness. It turned out that as he fell, he had hit his head on a window ledge and was knocked out. He told the newspaper that he recalled "waking up on the ground a little while later with a towel on my head, and people saying, 'you're going to be okay.'"

Safety on the Job

All construction jobs demand one thing of the worker and his or her employers: safety first. Although there are many priorities, including speed and quality of the work, safety is of the utmost importance. In an environment as unpredictable as a construction site, worker safety is never 100 percent guaranteed. It's not the sole responsibility of the bosses either. From the equipment manufacturers and the employers to the construction worker out on a steel beam or in a trench, safety is a team effort.

The Bad Old Days

Many years ago, the dangers involved in building projects were far worse than they are today. Part of the reason that there are fewer dangers is that over the years, the industry and workers have learned more about safety. In addition, workers pressed for a workday restricted to eight hours, which helped a great deal, as did better work conditions. It was only in the last few decades, however, that the federal government even

Before 1970, mandatory rules for things like safety harnesses did not exist. Here, a New York City construction worker, circa 1950, walks precariously across a steel girder. A sense of balance and agility are his only real protections.

started playing a big part in worker safety.

OSHA

In 1970, the Occupational Safety and Health Administration (OSHA) was created as part of the U.S. Department of Labor. OSHA helped bring to light a variety of construction-related hazards. As a result, machines with exposed moving parts were required to have guards put on them. Limits were established regarding the maximum amount of exposure workers could have to the six hundred or so chemicals that are used in the building industry. Later, OSHA set up certain rules and

Common pieces of protective equipment worn at a construction site are earmuffs, to protect against extremely loud noises, and heavy-duty gloves.

procedures for making sure energy sources and equipment were turned off safely. OSHA also defined rules for workers toiling in confined spaces, like underground tunnels or small passageways in buildings. These were places where dangers such as exposure to gases or injury were more likely.

Tools of the Trade

To help workers protect themselves from the unintended but very real dangers of their work environments, OSHA mandated the widespread use of personal protective equipment (PPE). PPE can be anything from a long-sleeved shirt to a sealed suit worn when removing hazardous materials. Gear includes goggles to protect eyes from flying sparks or other foreign objects. Depending on a worker's environment, laborers might need a respirator to protect their respiratory systems. Too much dust in the air or fumes from paint or from other chemical compounds can be harmful. Therefore, noses, lungs, and other breathing organs should not be exposed to the work conditions.

The list of potential hazards on a work site is long. Jagged nails and other sharp edges mean that a good, sturdy pair of gloves is needed. All the activity on a site can be confusing, and not everyone necessarily pays attention 100 percent of the time, although they should. Whether working on a highway or at a construction site, many employers make it a rule that their workers wear bright-colored, and thus highly visible, vests.

Wearing the proper boots is important, too. Shoes like flip-flops or sneakers won't cut it since they won't protect feet from falling tools or materials. Laborers also wear comfortable but snug clothing. Clothing that is too loose is dangerous because it can easily get caught on machinery or on the edge of other surfaces.

No matter what, the most important tool in a construction worker's arsenal is his or her head. That's why it is crucial to protect the head at all times in a work area. The typical protective head cover is a hard hat, or metal helmet. (In fact, some construction workers use "hard hat" as a nickname for someone in the industry.)

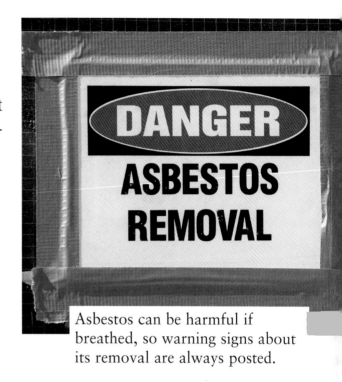

Asbestos can be harmful if breathed, so warning signs about its removal are always posted.

Asbestos and Other Inhalants

There are many building materials that can be harmful if breathed too much. One material is asbestos, a natural mineral made up of tiny, thin, long fibers. Now banned in construction, many old buildings still contain lots of it. When construction workers tear down or repair an old building, and break down walls and ceilings, they can release great amounts of asbestos. That's when laborers break out their filter masks, respirators, or gas masks.

SITE SAFETY NOTICE

Unauthorised entry to this site is strictly prohibited

WARNING CONSTRUCTION IN PROGRESS
Parents are advised to warn children of the dangers of entering construction sites

1. All visitors must report to the site office.
2. Permission must be obtained before entering the site or any work area.
3. Safety signs and procedures must be observed.
4. Personal protection and safety equipment must be used at all times.
5. All persons entering this site must comply with the regulations under the Health & Safety at Work Act 1974.

Safety helmets must be worn

Protective footwear must be worn

A sign with various warnings is a common posting at a construction site. Workers, visitors, and passersby all must be aware of the potential dangers of their surrounding environment.

With something like asbestos, it's not enough just to avoid breathing it in. Employers are required by law to help clean workers whose clothing is exposed to certain chemicals. When workers go home, they should avoid washing any of their construction gear with their normal clothes or with those of their family.

Safety, Safety, Safety

The unique job of construction laborers demands a unique approach to staying safe and keeping coworkers and friends safe, too. The preceding discussion of protective equipment falls into the "just-in-case" school of safety measures. Maybe you have heard the saying "an ounce of prevention is worth a pound of cure" or "the best defense is a good offense." In construction, these adages are something like a golden rule. Bosses, laborers, and the industry as a whole are always trying to think of better and additional ways to keep workers safe.

When it comes to workers' safety, too much is never enough. As sandhog Ken MacLean pointed out in *Lifelines* newsletter, experts predicted that Boston's "Big Dig" would claim the lives of more than 130 workers before it was done. From 1990 until its recent completion in 2007, however, only four people perished. He and others credit ever-improving safety measures. But, as MacLean points out, "that's four too many."

The Public Good

Construction laborers contribute much to the public good by building. They also have to be careful, however, that their work does the least harm possible to the general public. From minor complaints like the noise produced from using heavy machinery to extreme dangers like building and bridge collapses, whether construction is executed well or poorly can make a huge difference.

A Team Effort

Although OSHA has outlined rules on construction safety, the sheer number of construction projects means that it is hard for the government to investigate anywhere near as many work sites as it should. For the most part, employers keep things as safe as they can. Many do it out of a sense of morality; others do it because they do not want to deal with lawsuits from injured workers. But some do cut corners.

Workers can have a definite impact on their immediate work environment. Apprenticeships, classroom training, and learning on the job all give workers a background in safety. A simple rule of thumb is to use one's senses at all times. Seeing a threat is the most straightforward way of noticing a potential problem. But hearing someone's cry for help or a wall beginning to cave in, or smelling a strange smell that could be chemicals or the start of a fire—these are all essential for a laborer to be aware of.

Shock of a Lifetime

One of the biggest causes of accidents is simple forgetfulness or inattentiveness. This is often the case with electrocution, one of the most common—and preventable—hazards for laborers.

Especially when a building is still in its earlier stages, exposed wires or other dangers might exist. Workers should be positive that they have turned off all electrical equipment after using it. When operating tools near or around water or wet areas, it's always best to wear rubber gloves and boots—insulated materials that prevent electricity from harming the body.

A Long Way Down

Unsurprisingly, one of the other major causes of injuries and deaths is falls. Falling is probably the most immediate fear for a construction worker. Workers can fall off many different parts of a job site: the roof, scaffolding, or a ladder. One of the least expected ways of falling, though, is through a floor. Often, this will happen when one worker has moved a piece of plywood that was blocking a hole or empty section of floor. Another worker has no idea the board was removed and just happens to step through empty space where, moments ago, there was wood.

Thinking Long-Term

Workers also need to concentrate on details in order to prevent damage to their bodies over time. Spending years on the job, using many of the same tools, and performing tough physical labor can put great stress on the body. Laborers need to make sure they don't overexert themselves. That includes knowing

An iron worker carries equipment as he scales the steel column of a bridge section. In such an environment, a worker needs to be very aware of his or her environment because a misstep can mean serious or fatal injury.

how to properly lift something—using leg muscles rather than the back. Also, if workers know that they are going to be in a crouching position for a long time, it's probably best to pull up a seat and sit down. Even something as simple as balancing a tool belt helps; workers can develop muscle strains if they're carrying too much weight on one side of their body.

Thinking ahead will always beat looking back on what one should have done. Nothing good comes out of injuries that result in long-term pain, which could linger even after retirement. Working smarter now pays off tenfold in the future, and good construction workers learn this quickly.

A Profession Built to Last

As an industry, construction will only continue to grow. There will always be buildings going up. Old buildings, bridges, and tunnels will always have to be repaired or replaced. Building is simply one of the tools of human progress. Many construction workers enter the business because of their families. Some are even third or fourth generation construction laborers. Like firefighters and police officers, it is a kind of calling.

As much as we would like it to be, construction work will probably never be 100 percent safe. But if companies, unions, the industry itself, and individual workers keep it up, safety will only improve. Technology will give us some of the tools to save lives and prevent injuries. But it is the watchful eye of the worker

49

Marion Carnegie Library
206 S. Market St.
Marion, IL 62959

New York City: Snapshot of Construction Perils

In 2007, the *New York Times* reported that the construction industry was busier than ever. New York City, America's largest city, was no exception. With more buildings going up, though, it seemed that accidents increased as well.

According to a report by OSHA and the New York City Department of Buildings, accidents during the first eleven months of 2006 fell into several categories. Falls were the leading cause, accounting for about 51 percent of all accidents. Twenty-six percent of injuries resulted from falling materials. Equipment was responsible for 8 percent of accidents, while excavation was involved with 6 percent. Other assorted mishaps accounted for the remaining 9 percent of accidents.

The *Times* also reported that, while fatal accidents dropped from about twenty-five during 2002 to less than fifteen in 2003, they rose to twenty-nine in 2006.

City Hall News reported that a big reason for worker accidents and deaths was that employers, most of them nonunion companies, simply ignored the rules. OSHA estimated that about 86 percent of deaths occurred on nonunion jobs.

The mayor's office of New York, which established the Scaffold Worker Task Force in 2007, revealed that there are fewer skilled workers and fewer people looking out for them. In 67 percent of accidents involving scaffolding, for example, there was no supervisor on-site who was professionally licensed, as required by law. In addition, at least 50 percent of scaffold workers had not received a legally mandated training certificate to work on the scaffolding.

looking out for him- or herself and his or her coworkers that will always be the most important line of defense.

The job duties of construction workers may change in the future. The structures that will be built in the next decade or two no doubt will be larger and more ambitious than ever before. Materials and technologies will no doubt change and become more complex. The training and education for workers will have to keep up with these changes. One thing will never change, however. Men and women will continue to walk bravely across steel beams and scaffolds. People will brave the trenches or man the controls of awesome machines, helping to build the world a bit at a time. For them, it's all in a day's work.

Glossary

adrenaline A hormone that is produced by the body in response to stress or danger.

apprenticeship A job where someone works for a person or company for a certain amount of time to learn a trade.

aptitude A natural talent or ability.

asbestos A naturally occurring mineral once used widely in construction that has been largely banned but still exists in many old buildings. Workers exposed to it can suffer ill health effects.

contractors Individuals or companies with formal contracts to do specific jobs. They provide labor and materials, and any needed staff.

debris The broken remains of something destroyed; for example, the pieces of a building after it is torn down.

demolition The area of construction work dealing with tearing down buildings, especially old ones to be replaced with new ones.

flagger A highway construction worker who uses a flag to regulate traffic for the safety of both workers and motorists.

heavy equipment operator A construction worker who oper-
   ates large machines and vehicles.

hydraulic Refers to high-powered machinery that uses the
   movement of high-pressure fluids to create force.

lucrative Producing wealth or profit.

operating engineer A type of heavy equipment operator who
   is skilled in using several different kinds of machines.

personal protective equipment (PPE) Equipment used to protect workers from injuries and health problems. It includes
   protective clothing and devices that protect the head, eyes,
   and other vulnerable areas.

rope grab A safety device for construction workers working in
   an elevated location, it is a piece of line that attaches the
   worker to a main safety rope.

safety harness A piece of safety equipment that uses a series
   of straps wrapped around the worker's body to prevent him
   or her from falling from a height.

scaffold A temporary structure created to hold workers and
   their tools while working on a structure.

stamina The ability for someone to stand a great deal of
   physical exertion.

trench In construction, a hole dug in the ground that is usually
   deeper and longer than it is wide. Trenches are dug to
   install or repair infrastructure or to prepare foundations for
   structures.

utilities Government-regulated companies that provide services
   such as gas, electricity, or water.

For More Information

Associated General Contractors of America (AGC)
2300 Wilson Boulevard, Suite 400
Arlington, VA 22201
(703) 548-3118
Web site: http://www.agc.org
AGC is the largest and oldest construction trade association in
the United States.

**Canadian Centre for Occupational Health and Safety
(CCOHS)**
135 Hunter Street East
Hamilton, ON L8N 1M5
Canada
(905) 572-2981
Web site: http://www.ccohs.ca
The CCOHS is a branch of the Canadian government that
handles worker safety and works to eliminate work-related
illnesses and injuries.

Canadian Construction Association (CCA)
75 Albert Street, Suite 400
Ottawa, ON K1P 5E7
Canada
(613) 236-9455
Web site: http://www.cca-acc.com/home.html
The CCA advocates for the construction industry in Canada
and provides information and resources for builders.

U.S. Department of Labor
Bureau of Labor Statistics
2 Massachusetts Avenue NE
Washington, DC 20212-0001
(202) 691-5200
Web site: http://www.bls.gov/oco/cg/home.htm
The Bureau of Labor Statistics tracks statistics and trends for
jobs. Its career-guide page on construction is a valuable
resource for job descriptions, working conditions, and
other industry news.

U.S. Department of Labor
Occupational Safety & Health Administration (OSHA)
200 Constitution Avenue NW
Washington, DC 20210
(800) 321-OSHA (6742)
Web site: http://www.osha.gov

OSHA is the branch of the U.S. government in charge of preventing work-related injuries, illnesses, and deaths. It sets rules and standards for worker safety and conducts inspections to ensure compliance.

Web Sites

Due to the changing nature of Internet links, Rosen Publishing has developed an online list of Web sites related to the subject of this book. This site is updated regularly. Please use this link to access the list:

http://www.rosenlinks.com/exc/hrcw

For Further Reading

Apel, Melanie Ann. *Careers in the Building and Construction Trades* (Careers in the New Economy). New York, NY: Rosen Publishing, 2005.

Doherty, Craig A., and Katherine M. Doherty. *Hoover Dam* (Building America). Farmington Hills, MI: Blackbirch Press, 1995.

Green, Robert. *Construction* (Discovering Careers for Your Future). New York, NY: Ferguson Publishing, 2001.

Macaulay, David. *Building Big: Companion to the PBS Series.* Boston, MA: Houghton Mifflin, 2004.

Macaulay, David. *Underground.* Boston, MA: Houghton Mifflin, 1983.

O'Connor, Rachel. *Construction Worker* (High Interest Books). Danbury, CT: Children's Press, 2004.

Oxlade, Chris. *Canals* (Building Amazing Structures). Portsmouth, NH: Heinemann, 2005.

Pasternak, Ceel, and Linda Thornburg. *Cool Careers for Girls in Construction.* Manassas Park, VA: Impact Publications, 2000.

Richards, Julie. *Skyscrapers and Towers* (Smart Structures). North Mankato, MN: Smart Apple Media, 2003.

Stone, Lynn M. *Skyscrapers* (How Are They Built?). Vero Beach, FL: Rourke Publishing, 2001.

Wallner, Rosemary. *Construction Carpenter* (Career Exploration). Mankato, MN: Capstone Press, 2000.

Wilkinson, Philip. *Building* (Eyewitness Books). New York, NY: DK Children's Books, 2000.

Bibliography

Christie, Les. "America's Most Dangerous Jobs." CNN Money.com. August 17, 2006. Retrieved September 2007 (http://money.cnn.com/2006/08/16/pf/2005_most_dangerous_jobs/index.htm).

Coletti, Louis. "Construction Safety: A Tale of Two Cities." City Hall. April 17, 2007. Retrieved September 2007 (http://www.cityhallnews.com/news/129/ARTICLE/1165/2007-04-17.html).

Edwards, Kenneth. "Apprenticeships: Valuable Training for Higher-Paying Jobs." U.S. Air Force Library Education Resource Center. Retrieved September 2007 (http://www.petersons.com/cpc/career.asp?sponsor=3893&tab=articles&art=apprentice).

Fimrite, Peter, Matthew B. Stannard, and Jim Herron Zamora. "Napa Bridge Falls: Worker Killed, 7 Hurt in Sudden Collapse at Construction Site." *San Francisco Chronicle.* December 4, 2003. Retrieved September 2007 (http://sfgate.com/cgi-bin/article.cgi?f=/c/a/2003/12/04/BAGMU3FRVO1.DTL).

Garrity, Kathleen. "More Women Choose Construction."
    Seattle Daily Journal of Commerce. August 31, 2000.
    Retrieved September 2007 (http://www.djc.com/news/
    const/11113344).

Hedlund, Mark, and Elizabeth Bishop. "Construction Worker
    Rescued After Falling into Hole." ABC News 10. January 23,
    2007. Retrieved September 2007 (http://www.news10.net/
    display_story.aspx?storyid=23677).

Labors' Health and Safety Fund of North America. "Tunnel Work
    Booming, Safety Training Critical." *LifeLines Newsletter.*
    Winter 2006. Retrieved September 2007 (http://www.
    lhsfna.org/index.cfm?objectID=0200919A-D56F-E6FA-
    9FC1386D0464E8A8).

Marciano, Rob (correspondent). Transcript of CNN *American
    Morning* broadcast. CNN. August 7, 2007. Retrieved
    September 2007 (http://cnnstudentnews.cnn.com/
    TRANSCRIPTS/0708/07/ltm.02.html).

Meyer, Samuel W., and Stephen M. Pegula. "Injuries, Illnesses,
    and Fatalities in Construction, 2004." Bureau of Labor
    Statistics, U.S. Department of Labor. May 24, 2006.
    Retrieved October 2007 (http://www.bls.gov/opub/cwc/
    sh20060519ar01p1.htm).

Olesen, Alexa. "29 Killed in China Bridge Collapse."
    Time.com. August 14, 2007. Retrieved September 2007
    (http://www.time.com/time/world/article/0,8599,1652694,
    00.html).

Sandlin, Rebecca L. "Man Injured in Construction Accident." *Noblesville Daily Times.* September 5, 2007. Retrieved September 2007 (http://www.county29.net/cms2/index.php?option=com_content&task=view&id=5908&Itemid=1).

Shapiro, Nina. "Wanted: More Hard Hats." *Seattle Weekly.* March 3, 2004. Retrieved September 2007 (http://www.seattleweekly.com/2004-03-03/news/wanted-more-hard-hats.php).

U.S. Census Bureau News, U.S. Department of Commerce. "August 2007 Construction at $1,166 Billion Annual Rate." September 28, 2007. Retrieved October 2007 (http://www.census.gov/const/C30/release.pdf).

U.S. Department of Labor, Bureau of Labor Statistics. "Construction Laborers." Occupational Outlook Handbook. Retrieved September 2007 (http://www.umsl.edu/services/govdocs/ooh20022003/ocos248.htm).

Index

About the Author

Philip Wolny, a writer and teacher, was raised in New York City. As a teenager, he worked doing demolition on a construction site. He is currently completing a master's program in his native Poland.

Photo Credits

Cover © Michael Kertgens/VISUM/The Image Works; pp. 5, 48 © age fotostock/SuperStock; p. 7 © Sonda Dawes/The Image Works; p. 9 © www.istockphoto.com/Lisa F. Young; p. 11 © www.istockphoto.com/Sean Locke; p. 12 © Paul J. Richards/ AFP/Getty Images; p. 16 © John Berry/Syracuse Newspapers/ The Image Works; p. 19 © Jim West/The Image Works; p. 22 © David Bacon/The Image Works; p. 23 © www.istockphoto.com/ 314; pp. 24, 30 © AP Images; p. 27 © Robert A. Sabo/Getty Images; p. 32 © www.istockphoto.com/Anton Foltin; p. 35 © www.istockphoto.com/Frank Leung; p. 36 © Mark Wilson/ Getty Images; p. 40 © Ben McCall/FPG/Hulton Archive/Getty Images; pp. 41, 44 Shutterstock.com; p. 43 www.istockphoto.com/ Gord Horne.

Photo Researcher: Amy Feinberg